Loose Weather

LOOSE WEATHER

Poems by
Robert Herschbach

Washington Writers' Publishing House
Washington, D.C.

Copyright © 2013 by Robert Herschbach
All rights reserved

COVER ART *April Interstate*, 2013, by Christopher Volpe
AUTHOR'S PHOTO by Yihua Zheng
COVER DESIGN by Sid Gold and Barbara Shaw
TYPESETTING by Barbara Shaw

LIBRARY OF CONGRESS CATALOGUING-IN-PUBLICATION DATA
Herschbach, Robert, 1966-
 [Poems. Selections]
 Loose Weather : Poems / by Robert Herschbach.
   pages cm.
 ISBN 978-0-931846-70-0 (paperback : alk. paper)
 I. Title.
 PS3558.E7598L66 2013
 811'.54—dc23
                                             2013029865

Printed in the United States of America
WASHINGTON WRITERS' PUBLISHING HOUSE
P. O. Box 15271
Washington, D.C. 20003

For Yihua

Acknowledgements

Some of the poems in this manuscript originally appeared in the following publications, to which the author extends appreciation and thanks: *Eclipse*: "Dumplings"; *Fine Madness*: "Hampton in Winter"; *Fugue*: "Stopover"; *Gargoyle*: "Scottish Play"; *Grey Sparrow Journal*: "The Week of White Box Trucks"; *Mondo Greco*: "Sphinx"; *Natural Bridge*: "Infidelity"; *Painted Bride Quarterly*: "Michael: A Sequence"; *Pebble Lake Review*: "Cavafy's Theme"; *Puerto del Sol*: "Marina Tsvetaeva"; *Quarterly West*: "An Epic"; *Southern Poetry Review*: "At the Library, the Largest in Three States"; *Subtropics*: "Loose Weather," "Cul-de-Sac"; *The Ampersand Review*: "New Tenants in the Old Apartment"; *The Cafe Review*: "Cash," "Cove with Traveler," "Korean War Drill," "Lisa Dancing," "The Empire of Noon"; *The Country Dog Review*: "The Lycée Student"; *The Louisville Review*: "Siesta"; *The South Carolina Review*: "Appetite"; *The Sow's Ear Poetry Review*: "Komungo"; *West Branch*: "Kitchen."

"An Epic," "Minaret" and "Quintet" were part of the chapbook *A Lost Empire*, published in 1994 by Ion Books. "An Epic" also appeared in the anthology *Under the Legislature of Stars: 62 New Hampshire Poets* (Oyster River Press, 1999).

I would like to thank the many people who offered support and encouragement during the time these poems were written. I am particularly grateful to the teachers I have been privileged to study with, and to James Kimbrell, friend and mentor. Special thanks also to Barbara Campbell for the gift of her friendship and the inspiring example of her work, and to Elizabeth Antalek, Leonard Cushing, Shelley Girdner, Joshua Green and Julia Story.

This book would not have been possible without the efforts of Sid Gold, whose close editorial eye has strengthened many of the poems. Thanks also to Kathleen Hellen and Holly Karapetkova for their comments and suggestions, to Barbara Shaw for her design and typesetting skills, to Patric Pepper for shepherding the project through to completion, and to all the writers at WWPH.

I am indebted to Angela Ball for her generosity and insight, and to Christopher Volpe — painter and poet — for his artistic vision.

Love and gratitude to my parents, Dennis Herschbach and Mary Pittas-Herschbach, and to my sisters, Alissa and Elisabeth. Above all, I would like to thank my wife, Yihua Zheng, and my children, Heidi and Michael, for their love and support.

Table of Contents

I. *Poseidon Boulevard*
    Sphinx   3
    Hampton in Winter   4
    Athens, 1975   5
    Mother Tongue   6
    The Lycée Student   7
    Oil Portraits of a Wife   9
    Seraphs   12
    Scottish Play   14
    Stopover   15
    Cash   16
    Kitchen   17
    Poetry Radio Hour   20

II. *The Language Trade*
    Marina Tsvetaeva   25
    Port City Dive   26
    Eye Contact at Panmunjom   27
    Korean War Drill   28
    The Language Trade   29
    Komungo   30
    The Empire of Noon   31
    Cavafy's Theme   34
    Lisa, Dancing   35
    Cove with Traveler   37

III. *Daddy Paperclip*
    Loose Weather   41
    Cul-de-sac   42
    Infidelity   43
    Appetite   45
    At the Library, the Largest in Three States   46
    New Tenants in the Old Apartment   47
    Dumplings   48

Lego Man	49
Lego Bride	50
Lego Mama	51
Town of Smooth Surfaces	52
Brickocalypse	53
The Week of White Box Trucks	54
Michael: A Sequence	55

IV. *Augury*

The President of Regrets	63
The President of Sleep	64
The President of Augury	65
The President of Sweet Nothings	66
An Epic	67
Minaret	70
Quintet	74
Siesta	78
Silence	80

I.
Poseidon Boulevard

Sphinx

Someday I'm going to wake up
and not be able to see
out of my eyes, which are stone,
or move my hands, which are fish.

The barbed wire caught in my lip.
The skin washing ashore like sheets
of plastic. And the tin can
in my head, empty.

One of these days the Jew's harp
in my throat will snap, just as I thought
I finally had it — the answer

to the Sphinx, and the other riddle
where legs are strings, and we fiddle.

Hampton in Winter

The arcades shut, bikers gone.
No more water nymphs
cruising the boardwalk
in fluorescent swimwear.
Just the smell of old batter
in a street of padlocked stores,
flyers still tacked to posts.
Gnats in a nuptial dance
by the burger joint,
closed for the season.
Sun like a white hole-punch
in a well-thumbed sky.

I stopped here on a whim
that now slips off
like a deceptive ghost,
leaving this bare beach,
the horizon's freighters
and the notorious island,
site of a thieves' colony…

Cold tones, busy sea,
some longing I carry around
like a penny, gummy and dark.

Athens, 1975

Reports say don't swim in the waters
off Poseidon Boulevard,
but tell that to matrons
wearing Jackie O shades,

husbands with the look of colonels
after the coup failed.
They don't believe the sea
will hurt them

or that the factory around the cape
hurts the sea. They cup it
onto their bodies,

unable to loosen
the knot of grudges

or pick the right saint
from the lineup — twenty martyrs,
each with a cure for something.

The air cools. A car horn answers Dixie
to another's Marseillaise.
Athens continues,
but in the way of a daughter
in a shocking dress.

Already the young are out
breaking records, chasing
planes on mopeds — every other word they say
a blasphemy.

Mother Tongue

Don't speak English, my sisters said
as we snuck by the news kiosk
placed like a chess piece
at the corner. We did not want to be known

as others. Balconies all around us,
verandahs and open windows.
Families whose talk would hush
to keen hearing

as we went by. *Xenoi.*
Amerikanoi. One sister
olive-toned and dark of eye

as any Ionian girl. The other
almost blonde, a California cherub.
Both fluent in our mother's tongue,
which impatience kept me
from learning.

Evenings, the soccer ball
we kicked around was dusty
as the street. We played freeze tag

in alleys where stray cats
nursed their litters. Shouting as
kids do, but never in English.

Land of Evel Knievel and the cruise
missile, purple mountains majestic,
suburbs from sea to sea,

you were just too big
to belong to.

The Lycée Student

Late to join the bell-summoned line
of kerchiefs and caps,
she looks out from the foreground

as though to make contact
with us, the outside-the-painting
people. As though she'd like to play hookey

here for a spell, leaving her classmates
to trip over names they must learn:
Daladier, King Zog…

A curious encounter. She
as yet unaware of A or H-bombs,
the camps and the trains,

Europe busting apart like statuary
dropped from a height, or an Egypt
without Greeks, her people.

And us not knowing
how to break the news, explain
the way we live now, logged on

and locked down. How to gloss
words like *fracking*
or *killbox*, not in any lingo

she'd have taken to heart.
Back turned to the others
posed in various attitudes,

she must stay at the threshold
where the artist put her,

pictured as innocence —
delight in her expression like a child's
when promised the movies.

Oil Portraits of a Wife

1.

She lives among her likenesses
in an Athens apartment,

a clique of former selves
painted by her beau
when Art and Love were all,

before he left *la vie bohème*
for Delphic Advertising, Ltd
and bought a car
the color of his shaving cream.

Neighborhood beauty, fiancée,
new wife darning a scarf —
but none of her in robust

middle age, back from market
and a stop at church. She halves apricots,
sets water to boil, feeds the stray cats

mincemeat or anchovies,
top-dollar scraps. When she enters the living room
the versions of her smile
amiably. They are sanguine

young women, if ill-informed.
Thinking luscious curls
will see them through all trouble.

2.

They charm visitors
like polite younger sisters
who understand when not to speak.

Cousins who have aged
with her bear witness.
She did not look so intense.
The cast of her face a little off…
Her eyes were green, yes, but differently.

Back from London or the States,
her children shrug. They did not
know her then.

Must she endure
comparisons, this searching
of her face for pretty ghosts,

and the shameless way her husband
shares his ardor

with a dozen women
of his own creation,
calling it fidelity?

3.

Still, the silken afternoon
is hers to relish. A tin bearing a pasha's image
yields Turkish delight, violet
and lavender, confectioner's sugar
powdering her fingertips.

My mind is going, I am old,
she confides, stumped
by the daily crossword
and demoiselles on the wall

who practice their manners
and don't talk back. Discreet,
they wait for her return
from the verandah

where twice a day she smokes
a private cigarette.

She could tell them what the end
of youth is like,
but they'd only hear her as their mother
coming from the evening liturgy,
perplexed by bells and frankincense,
the priest's warnings.

They have no time for that.
They are busy naming the beasts,

tending large, improbable flowers
that bend towards them,
purring.

Seraphs

The priest, his voice like an oboe,
spoke of compassion, the lamb
and the knife, the library wing
our good urges wrote checks for.

I wasn't good. I was twelve,
and girls my age wore their hair big,
chose Sunday dresses with tiny clasps
at the back, their fashions wrapping them up

for display, like fruit or chocolate. White flowers
grew in the Savior's wounds, a saint
tore off his arm to show the flesh
meant nothing, and all I could think of
was Daphne Rouvelas,

her miraculous skin tone,
what her lips might feel like. Why didn't God
strike me dead? He was the king

said to be in the building
while his adorers wait. Taking his own
sweet time. If he knew all
he must also know

I couldn't help it. Who could be pure
in a place like this, all myrrh
and perfume, gold shining
in the churchy dark,
such sensuality
in the name of the spirit?

Above us all, seraphs in the dome
wore wings fancy as boas, and the sun beamed in
at an angle, making a bath of light

for a martyr's feet. The priest
stopped talking, began to sing.
At the end, we stood in line
to coat our tongues with a syrupy wine
and grab fistfuls of good Greek bread.

Scottish Play

The drama club is rehearsing
the end of kings — bloodied iambs
on teenagers' lips,
lies and seduction.
Fog effects, pink-toned dry ice,
grunt of the queen
as she urges on
the essential deed: a king dies. Twice.
It comes with the job.

Everything the king says
is addressed to the dagger
and poison, ghosts
he births in his spare time
or the weird sisters Brianna,
Marissa and Caitlin
whose riddles he must complete.

The queen's hunger
makes geometry worth it,
the smell of a lunchroom microwave
or old socks in gym class
bearable for her sake,

but the queen grows mad
with consequence
and the slave who must pay
has not even one line
for his trouble.

Stopover

The perky scarf comes off, the airline pin,
the royal blue you used to think
would change you,

June from Delaware,
lost among hotel room pastels,
imaginary woodlands.

At the foot of the bed, the prim tote
you drag past news and food
in Hartford, Duluth, Tulsa…
all those towns where people live.

The others down in the piano bar
— you wanted to be alone tonight
with your fantasy captain,

he of the level gaze and Viking's build,
dead last year in an Arctic fireball.
Tonight you're his dream stewardess,

dispensing orchid scents
as you glide up and down the cabin,
permanent personal air machine
fanning your hair.

Flush with the glamour
of networks, glow-in-the-dark routes
that curve over poles and oceans.

Serene, like the ladies
nailed to the fronts of ships
in olden days.

Cash

It can stink like old shoes,
curl at the edges, be a face
gone ragged and creased.
It's still tender. A machine
may not take it but somebody will.

The job's gone, plastic expired,
but a pocket in the clothes-heap
yields its folded promise:
you won't end this night
hungry or sober. Fries oiling the paper,
the haddock snug in its batter,
the too-sweet wine that will have to do
greeting your lips like a sloppy kiss…
Cash is the invite to such a feast.

It bears your prints, the residues
of touch. No other approval needed,
nothing to swipe or sign.
Though the world's poker faced
behind aces and queens,
you've got a trick up your sleeve —
the moment yours to spend.

Kitchen

1.

Rice scatters. There are nooks
under stoves, and spaces
for stray grains where things —
wood, formica — come together.

My grandmother spooned rice
into yogurt cups,
then she'd tip them
over our plates. Rice castles.
The fun was in knocking them down.

2.

Potatoes of the sky
fatten up, darken.
This is in Holland.
Gaunt farmers stoop
to enter stone cottages.
A pregnant wife
sits on a table,
cooling her buttocks.
Nearby, a minister
reads from a starchy Bible.

3.

Thumb-like clove,
the flat side of a knife
split your casing — now you wait
on the cutting board
among diced onions,
tomatoes. Truth
is bald and cold.

Thrown into the pan,
you marry the olive,
fill a whole house
with the news,
turn my mouth into
a hothouse for strange,
toxic flowers. Later
I'll sleep like a body
buried in a garden.

4.

New Year's Eve
and Mother used to throw
a plate out the front door.
Bad luck if it didn't break,
so she'd choose carefully,
this gift for the dead year.
In the morning,
sweeping the shards
from the walk,
I'd think about
ghost plates, piling up
in the spirit pantries.
For what grand occasion?

5.

Where I live now, distinctions
are crisp — one night
frogs shrill, the next they don't.
Just like that, it seemed,
the tree in the kitchen's view
turned spare and pronged,
a distant cousin to the fork.
One ill-fitting window keeps
a whole room on edge,
the draft like bad mail
as I stir tonight's carrots,
simmering them until tender
in thyme and vinegar.

Poetry Radio Hour

In the scented stupor of August,
dazed as though from noontime sleep,
I'd climb past stilts to visit my friend

who didn't drink, up in his boat cabin
above a garage. Water
was our hourglass, ice melting
in the dollar-store pitcher.
                      In his kitchenette,
among quotables pinned to cork,
a well-coiffed Anne Sexton
fingered her neck, looking
slightly amused. Strange it seemed
not to pop open beers,

not to ride that lurching cable car
with its piney view,

not to get buzzed. As though fallen out
of some game board box,
colored chips urged him on
from sofa and rug, while a cat
warmed old paperbacks.

We listened to poetry on the radio,
our teacher drawling his way through
an anthology piece

in a voice aged fifty-two years
by Irish distillers. He and my friend and I
and Anne Sexton might have been
part of a cabal,

mystic order of the loft, yard sale soirée,
and anything, it seemed, could harbor
beauty and truth —

cars in the weeds, a stretch of track
with its wildflowers and tar,
or even the dead downtown,
liquidation sale stickers
igniting the windows.

II.
The Language Trade

Marina Tsvetaeva

I saw her name
on the hull of a cargo ship
docked in Pusan.
Its crew gone to the sex bars
north of the train station —
transactions of weariness and need
in a broken language.

Marina. Utopia cast her out
like the village witch,
starving her in a boondocks,
her poems a secret
no one must utter. *My unearthly home.*
Now she ferries containers,
spare parts, seven syllables of reverie

stamped on black steel.
The men return, stone-faced
and groggy. Vladivostok-bound,
she lifts anchor again,
beelines past refineries, cranes
dangling their question marks.
Open sea, exile's afterlife.

Port City Dive

Each night, unsure of their land legs,
the crews swagger or stumble, teased
by the high-kicking neon cowgirl
and her wink. Looking for a sailor's share
of bliss, trouble worth coming ashore for.
Auntie sells them Korean flags,
bowing like a monk before each table.

Hookers work the john. They'll size you up
for free. The Russians shout names
at the fancy dancer as she spins
by the wallpaper waterfall. *Anya,
Luba, Valentina.* In each man's heart a room
where once he built a model ship,
wishing himself at the wheel.

The ashen-faced one sums up the ports
he's been drunk in, names of lost loves.
He can say "sweet thing" in Thai, Lao, Bahasa —
and knows this place just plays at sin,
compared to some. Twenty years, he says,
since his calling came for him
and he stole away to meet it, no qualms or tears,
turning his back on the lie of home.

Eye Contact at Panmunjom

Face cut by the wind
he stood guard in, a soldier
leered at us through the glass
as though we were apes
dressed up for his amusement.

I remember the red star
on his hat, lean features
under the furred edge,
that look which could have been
taunt or grimace. As we moved
through the room, with its mikes set out
for invisible envoys, its small flags
that children could wave at a fair,
he goaded us to respond,
as we'd been told not to do.

He was scarcely farther away
than a friend might have been,
opposite me at some table,
lifting his shot glass in a toast.
I'd like to say I saw brotherhood
in his gaze, a flare of rapport,
but that would be more wish than truth
in a land of halves, the space
between us tense as a rope.

Korean War Drill

Parked like an audience
in front of changing lights,
traffic waits. Even freight ships
are still, as though pinned to the bay.

Like the strange insistent cry
of an all-devouring bird,
police whistles stop time.
Those in the shops must stay there,
confined among stationery, bras
or baguettes. Those outside must go in.

And now, just as we start
thinking it won't, the rehearsal
for emergency ends: we can resume
our trajectories. A tower crane
draws a curve in the sky. Dyed hemp flows
through human hands, into the lives of fish.

The Language Trade

Below the school window
a man is singing of jeans,
his cry a continuous loop,
come, see, buy. And they do,
the roaming brotherhoods,
arm-in-arm sisters, bank tellers
released from their windows.

A river of hips bears names,
stolen or misspelled,
platform shoes lift their wearers
to a higher realm, and I know
desire is what keeps me
climbing the stairs
to the heaven of English
where any girl can be Whitney,
Britney, Mariah. It's my job
to distribute idioms,
only the best and freshest,
the interview nailers,
the test high-scorers,

and I'm happy to be
your stand-up *meeguk,* smiling
like the golden age of TV,
feeding you jokes that fly
when half-understood. Six shows
each day, a funfair of language,
until the last class ends
and the bus carries me to the margins,
that vendor's cry twined
with my own shtick, turning
words into dough.

Komungo

The zither's a box for cries
suppressed. Six strings,

a bamboo stick, hands
in furtive telegraphy.

Somewhere outside
the annals, a poplar
stirs in noon heat.

In a side room of the palace,
a servant runs a cloth
across her body,

talking to no one.

The Empire of Noon

1.

The blonde above the record store
looks wan and sensual
or wan, starving and cold,
depending on the light.

Nude but for designer underwear,
she hugs her bony knees.
A campaign's afoot to bring her down,
this foreign goddess, lonesome
and immodest…

2.

Ships that brought war
also brought bread,

a word from Portugal — *pao,*
pang in Korean. And the thing

itself is altered in translation,
sour added to sweet, pickles

topping golden cakes,
bean tucked in an envelope

of flaking dough. Behind the door,
in an embroidered cap

reading *Mozart,*
a woman turns a key.

How swiftly the bakery shelves
make room for sunlight.

3.

A dozen Benzes
parked in the small lot,
inches apart.
And one shy valet,
sweating in his uniform,

armed with a dust cloth.

4.

Next year's bank tellers
wear sailor suits
and regulation bowl cuts.
The class leader waits
with scissors.

But nothing holds them
back at noon — all at once
they rush the gate.
Out for fishmeal on a stick,
the game arcades, lunchtime
karaoke,

screaming *we belong to
you and me.*

5.

Traffic eases down
the main drag.
From a cab's open window
comes a music of flutters
and sobs — reproach,
affection, lovers meeting
again in old age…

Above the rooftops
the clouds are like schooners.

For a quarter-hour I sit
on the steps outside
the museum of birds —
just for the feeling
of being somewhere.

Cavafy's Theme

Excess crowds out grief,
so let there be more
counterfeit jeans,
more girls just out of school,
taller than their mothers,
regulation bowl-cuts turned
to ringlets, improbable mauves…

More aromas of street food,
burnt silkworm, scallion pancake.
Always more music — transfigured, automated,
broadcast with watch-like precision
from subway platforms, department
store lobbies, from elevators everywhere.

And should you find yourself
greedy for ambience
melancholic and profound,
there is that too — late,
neon turned off, carts locked
and trundled away, a wail rises
from some basement karaoke.

Lisa, Dancing

Taller than the men who chased
the crescent moons
that fell from the strobe,

you made the dim club
worth its cover charge, punctured
drunken brains with shards
of jade, turned a port pagan.

Imperial frigates ablaze, death face
of a sunken king — to watch you
was to believe auburn ringlets
could rule a world, spinning
like beaded whips.

No doubt that night's cabs
took visions of you
to many beds,

and no doubt dancing sailors
chose crass words to forget you with,
failing every time.
                        Do you ever
think of them now, in your new guise
as good citizen,

cutting out shapes of states
for first graders, teaching
the moon's phases or the life cycle
of moths? Far from any harbor
starred with bordello lights,

does memory surprise you
with strange food,
a combustion of silkworms,

or conjure you again
as a many-armed goddess
among a retinue of eager men?

Cove with Traveler

The women divers of Korea
are out in the cove, surfacing
and disappearing again
among bobbing styrofoam
coolers. Near the bleached weights
piled on the dock, hemp nets
dry in the sun. Folk song's
coming across a bullhorn
on a truck parked in the sand…
You wanted to be somewhere else,
and you are. What's not to like?
Still, you keep looking out
across the bay to that *other*
tapering peninsula, the next one,
as though it's home
to further marvels — a rare
bird, a village on stilts,
the oldest cast-iron bell
in the hemisphere — the best
of all sights, the one thing
you don't want to miss.

III.
Daddy Paperclip

Loose Weather

Early spring's all flux and squalor —
here's a sole, far from its shoe.
Here's plastic sheeting in a dance
against the fence,
as one warped board
pulls out its nails.

Collecting orange peel
and tissue from the fallen bin,
I get a chill in my knees.
Above me, red husks
have broken on the pussywillow.
The furry catkins thumb forth,
rabbit's-foot soft.

Cul-de-sac

It's the hour of mail. Red flags stand at attention.
A passing car sheds bass notes,
mirrors hung on a branch
dizzy a lawn. Next door's gardener
comes out to talk to her flora —
see, she is bending to say something
only they can hear.
Drooling onto my shoulder,
the baby tears a leaf,
points at a plane, at a day moon.
Her life: things she can grab,
things out of reach.

At dusk the cul-de-sac is a rink
for shadows, but now it only lassoes
heat. A tricycle glows in a driveway. The boy
at the portahoop — sleeveless Pistons tee
glued to his back — shoots, scores.
Trombones of sunlight. And now
the mail comes, bringing ads and bills.

Infidelity

Same chain, different store —
the order of goods reversed,
light bulbs where the pasta should be,

steaks instead of juice. Checking
for landmarks — bakery, pharmacy —
you're startled by sushi-to-go,

braids of garlic among fat tomatoes,
yellow tomatoes, balloons
tethered to a rack of breads,

the automated downpour
that freshens the greens. Everything
comes from somewhere, small print

on a sticker. Far away, olives are pressed
and locusts whir. Hands you know
nothing of fill crates with clementines,

pack the meats, steer the big rigs
through the mountain gap
and all you have to do is choose.

Buy scents and suds, live on
Emerson Ave or Quiet Star Drive,
check the deck for loose nails.

What if you'd married the woman
in aisle five — all that coppery hair let loose
in a bedroom not unlike yours…

Her toddler swings his legs, points
and keeps repeating something urgently
incomprehensible. The muzak's

some old standard rescored for flute.
Back home, your own family waits,
a tableau turned at a slight angle.

Appetite

Some gulls are hood ornaments
on streetlamps. Others,
perchless, loiter among
the umbrellas — almost tame,
almost like dogs wanting scraps.

People, facing the sea
as though at a ball game,
seem to be waiting for something —
some wholeness, maybe,
that could take us back in.
It won't be this roil and suck,
pitchy as root beer,
the current a hook for showoffs.

Up on the boardwalk,
tattoos hail each other in passing,
bare feet take turns with a spigot.
Perhaps a beach is to happiness
as fried dough is to cuisine,
but I'm hungry. Above me
a man-made moth,
wings a pattern of flames.

At the Library, the Largest in Three States

Tired-looking women
waited for terminals
as a man cursed

up and down the line,
you eat me
alive, bitch.

Across the table, a reader
mouthed what his finger traced
in a large illustrated Bible.

I watched him for awhile,
then stared out past the railing
into the grand rotunda,

its walls stained blue
by the faint, medieval light
falling from a dome

invisible from this vantage point.

New Tenants in the Old Apartment
for Suzanne

They'll break it in like jeans,
the fit uncomfortable at first.
The hall too long for ease,
but perfect for fights, sleeping
at opposite ends.

They'll peel garlic, stir salt,
bag bottles. Wrap cut toenails
in tissue, relics not to be saved.
They'll find the best window

for daffodils, and the room
where nothing thrives.
On wet afternoons they'll hear
the guitar across the creek —

Jimmy Page in a basement,
no music exec around to catch
his riff. In June electric storms
will raise their hair. The landlord,
failing again to fix
the bad bathroom tap,

will tell his pet joke. They'll forgive him,
after enough of that lush red wine,
on sale down the street.

Some days it won't be enough
as dolor takes the shine
out of chairs, and hungry silences
eat their words. Distance
surprising them, like a house ghost.

Dumplings

Half-moons
on the cutting board,
rustic jewelry —

a hole at each end
to run a string through.

Coin purses,
each with its little offering.
Envelopes to be opened
after goodbyes,

on some night
when absence
keeps stealing the chairs,

when switching on lights
makes things darker still.

Wearing gloves
of flour, daughter and mom
tame the mountain in a bowl.
A calendar of dumplings:

how many a child
can eat in a night,

how much time they can buy
with work of the hands.

The smell of chives
gets into everything,
like the touch
of a friendly god.

Lego Man

I awoke holding a wrench.
Stubble and an eye-patch remained

from my life as a pirate.
I fit in everywhere I went:
Hard hat, top hat, cowboy hat.

Horse or jeep. A monkey
for my sidekick, or a droll dump truck.

My nature was to be of use.
Many jobs required only a fixed expression,
a stance among objects —

still, my head could turn
like a globe, my arm spin.
If demons were called for, I could flee.
If the city was doomed, I could be herald,

witness, the odd survivor
smiling under the rubble,
face polished as a lie.

Lego Bride

Her hair is borrowed. Her face
can be exchanged, scowl for smile.

Husband headless at the moment
while the child considers —

ambulance, safari, building site?
She falls apart so easily,

as though recombination
were her nature. She knows the dolor

under a bed, has bitten the heel
that would crush her,

suffers from nightmares
of swirling water. Build her a window.

Pose tulips in her flowerbed, an eager dog,
shine a flashlight and call it sunrise.

Lego Mama

All her babies are immaculate
and will never age.

Popsicle stick man,
Daddy Paperclip —

their ukulele tunes don't fool her —
she's immune to swagger

lacking dimension.
She wants her arm repaired,
fingers that move. Wants to throw the bird,

shoot a finger gun, make a fist
or here's-the-steeple.

Her babies are miniature Buddhas,
shiny rubbable bellies,

and her pets grin
like no animal should.

Her roofs
vanish like her men,
without notice.

Town of Smooth Surfaces

A diner without smells, omelets
you can't break with a fork, salt that won't spill
for bad luck. A park whose birds
never crap on the statues and cars.
A mayor given to silence.

The trains run on time. Buildings are vivid as ink,
garages grime-free. Residents stand in place
for hours, like generals awaiting
their parade, then fall to kiss the floor.

God's a pair of hands, the fingers
squirming with intent, flying down out of nowhere
to place a stop sign on the road,
wreck a wall. Capricious
hands. If they want a pirate crew
in the hospital or a helicopter
carrying zebras, this world will accommodate.

Brickocalypse

The town has always known
it's not for real. People lose their heads
with ease. The water tower keeps up appearances.

A day of heave-ho
brings a dusk of soaps and scents.
So I was promised. They posed the goodie bags
on trees.

We'll never know who set the moon
to plunder offices,
a ravenous wrecking ball
loving walls to death. Now the talking tractor bares its teeth,
the robots mutiny.

I go looking for a peg to plant my feet on,
a reason for the Santa
hanging off a bridge,
all this colorful rubble.

Batteries full, a train
keeps rounding the catastrophe
as though nothing special has happened.

The Week of White Box Trucks

If we noticed them before,
it was in the vague way we know
of slaughterhouses or hands
busy in granaries. Now no parking lot was safe
and the logos of giant stores
wouldn't help us.

Looking for cover, we found trajectories:
anyone could die hauling lumber
or cookware, trunk
open like a grave.
The crosshairs of the possible
fixed us at the gas pump
and its spinning numbers: click.
Our own lives setting us up
for the quick kill.

Who would have thought
so many windowless boxes
wheeled around us,
blank but for "wash me"
fingered in the grime?
What relief when the leads
turned false,

and we could see them
once again as nothing more
than ambulances
for mundane needs —
fish on ice, furniture
in bubble wrap,
hardwood for our floors.

Michael: A Sequence

1.

A paperback alien, he radiates
swimming-pool green,
glowing through his wraps.
The cable, strange tail,
spirals to a box on the floor.
My wife gives him milk
and he steeps her in light.
We study his skin tone.
I press my finger and see,
letting go, how red rushes back in.
He's like an unbalanced photo,
the color mix off. A small risk,
it sends us to wait among
calendars of encouragement,
babies dressed up as bugs.
Blind, unaware of the world
as object, he can't see them, or us —
pain is a prick to the heel,
a count done daily
until the number is right.

2.

Deng is the word
from his mother's tongue, first word
he speaks, meaning powers that shine
out of reach, couch-side
or above —

light makes the world
and he wants us to be
the makers of light.
The match sets a genie to dance
on the wick tip, white shells
plug the mouths
in the walls where *deng* lives

and someone left the moon on in the day,
wasting electricity. Wails
one evening: the candelabra's twin
speaks tongues in the window

and later we find our boy
mulling dark, a box of it
over his head, the vent grille
the thinnest of shields.

3.

In a city of timed lights
engines idle while we cross,
big-eyed traveler
holding your floppy toy,
your cuddly toothless dog.
It is a way to make you sleep —
push you among sights
until your brain dizzies and tires.
We have watched the water cathedral
build and dismantle itself,
and the glass elevator
rise like a float. Out in the park,
people behind a table are shouting
at people in general, the mass of us
crossing through, ignorant
of the Libya connection,
the submerged funds, the blood-for-bridges
secret deal. We have seen fish
in a window, taxi lamps
riding traffic, benevolent bread
on a sign we pass under.
For now it is all
yours to grin or cry at
or shut your eyes to.

4.

He could not yet walk
that time you flew away
and at night, moving on knees,
he guided his dump truck
through the rooms — upstairs,
downstairs, until he was tired.
Where was Utah? What did
nine days mean? You were
somewhere past the water tower,
the sky was hiding you.
Plane, day-moon,
wisp of cloud — you were a voice
in a toy held to his ear,
telling him to be good.

When what you want
is out of reach, clean house,
a friend told me once.
Garden or cook,
find something to sweep —
our hands make us believe
the world can be grasped. Today
he loads the truck with soil,
carts it to the flowerbed:

I am doing a job.
The pinwheel-turned-plow
rests on its side —
he won't let anyone move it.

5.

Displacement's the default,
every noun a verb
at slow speed. Slides,
swings addle him: he needs rungs.
Sister's inside, then outside
mother. A twist of scarlet
whirls in the marble's ocean.

Moon in the sky, on the staircase,
crescent-shaped scratch
guarding a step. World at a tilt.
He can believe leaves grow
into trees, or the robin's belly
harbors a fridge egg —
nothing that couldn't be true.

IV.
Augury

The President of Regrets

1.

Putting his pen to the bill,
cocking the gun of state, it's his job
to sigh and sign. His is the letter
from a fourth grade girl,
daddy's pink slip attached.
His the poison forest, the fallen pier.

Microphones in Russian fur hats
broadcast his grief. More towns die.
He looks for redemption,
finds only advisors.

2.

Who knows the land as he does? He has shared
waffles with farmers, slept in the corn,
imbibed the drawl. The votes were like applause

that night of his triumph, when all his jokes
hit home. Now he's a four-letter word
in the mouths of good citizens,

a bad vibe at the Bowl-o-Rama,
an autograph framed on the wall
of a diner that closed.

When can he feel anonymous again
in any neighborhood?

The President of Sleep

A nation of insomniacs —
up shuffling loan terms, refiguring
the retirement. Parking the skid steer
after the late shift. Driving big rigs
through downpours of sulfur.

Snug as a pear in foil,
the dozing president maintains a smile.
Sailing in the schooner of his ease,
the chief executive of slumber
knows the sirocco and meltemi,
familiar spirits. Like an aquarium
his dreaming mind is home
to quick-moving forms, warm colors.

Deep breather-in-chief. Head
of the bed. Wooing the Lorelei
perched on a rock.
He sleeps for all of us
who pick-axe the night
for coal, clean the machines,
or guard the marbled lobbies
of always-lit buildings.

The President of Augury

He climbs out from under his desk,
wearing a miniature violin on his lapel.
We elected him fortune teller-in-chief,
palm reader to the stars, America's soothsayer.

He opens his mouth: nothing.
He is stricken as though by a nude
feeling herself up in the corner. *Time to leave*,
murmur the handlers,
guiding us to chandeliers
in the Green Room. *Please
drop your questions into this lacquered box.*

Knowing we're hurt
but not the cause, we go home
to greet our fears, waiting for us like the mail.
The bombs disguised as seed,
the fatal water in our taps…

Time to resume punching buttons,
hauling rivets, driving spikes
into trees, whatever it takes

for a life of beer and pancakes
in the little towns reporters love.

The President of Sweet Nothings

He's building a cottage of lies for you,
in a wood of candied trees. He has a golden nickel,
a saddle, a porcelain horse that talks.

He's king of the jukebox. He has one in his room,
with your favorite song. And your second favorite.
Won't you come up and slow dance
under the stick-on stars?
The president's got rhythm,
you can tell the press later,
all eyes on your hickey.

No one believes you when you tell them
about his hands — how they are velvet curtains
opening to marvels. His words
emcee even the plainest moment,
locating the pathos in breakfast,
the comedy in a summer cold.

He's building. One ice cube at a time.
He's pasting windows
on a cottage. Promising sugar
and limitless oil, kissing diplomacy's cheeks.
He's manufacturing forests for you,
glitter-dipping the popsicle sticks.

And when you have him alone,
drinking him in like sherry
after a long day, he'll lean close
to whisper: *Dearest,*
our lives are too brief for truth.

An Epic

My liege, this is a brittle place.
Cortez, with his excellent nose
Sniffing out no scent of gold
Would surely have passed it over.
And the pink dogs pawing at tubers,
The pink bellied dogs

Mounting each other from boredom…
The sky like lacerated flesh.
We went to the creek,

Which was heaving up fish. They were
A marvel, for they had no eyes or scales,
But were rubbed into pale, indeterminate
Shape. They fell apart in my hands.
And my liege, he said: find the red root.
And six of them held me down, reached
Into my mouth. And my liege, he said:
Find the magic acorn. He held
The penknife to the soft, pink flesh
Of my ear, and I was afraid.

And he said: do not fear, for we are all
Blessed by the golden hands of the sun.
And he held up the ear, like a moist fungus.
Look how nature has blessed us, he said.

———

Cortez, his face like jagged rock.
His shoes, two slabs of blackened
Meat, breaded with dust. The equation
He carries in his head

Goes something like this: if x is the modest
Wingspan of days, and y cramps us
Into its nook, if the bigger half
Of the wishbone equals the better part
Of mercy, if the number of stones
Weighing me down shall determine
How quickly I learn to swim,

Then what use dreaming

———

Of cool terraces, bare feet
On marble? And the well-fashioned
Sandal? And the wicker chair
To act as a frame

For constantly shifting thighs
And bellies, intertwining laughter?
Sticky as a damp sheet was the air.
The moon like a huge vitamin,
Undissolved

In the night's throat.
My long hair like a curtain.
He opened it, and my face
Was bald in the halflight,
A lump of white putty.

His fingers rolled back
The sleek cords, in his hands
My head was a rounded globe
On which he traced cities,
Canals. Do not fear, he said,
We are all already

Absolved, even now
Somebody's clammy fingers
Are sponging the page…

Minaret

Don't forget the camellias,
She said, or the tongue in your mouth
That turned to glass

When you tried to speak, that dissolved
In water. You want to swallow
The past like a capsule, spreading
Ink through veins

Of a leaf until you are marble.
But camellias, and the serious look

Of an eight year old practicing piano scales.
And girls in the courtyard, singing
"Princess Tatiana." Never forget
The stem, the stake in your heart
That pins you forever.

———

The scent was of lemon trees,
But how you would like to believe
It was their voices, transmuted, picked up
By the breeze.

———

Don't forget the ghost of a smirk haunting
The courtesan's face

In the mosaic, as if to say "They jailed me
Here — how about you?" The sandals
Of those who walked in the above
World, Constantinople. You

Who listen to rustle of leaves and hear
Tambourines, or booty of coins, or sea,
Do not forget the medallions that made
Holy the wrist of Madame, her finespun soul,
Circumscribed by no time or place, staring
At you from inside the painted cage
Of her face. *Learn to inhabit the split seam
Of what and why*, she said,

Placing the cards face down on the table.
You turned one over, and there you were,
Leapfrogging into the sun. And there
You were, nailed up to the sky with stars.
Never forget, she said, *what night heals,
Day reopens*. And the muezzin,

Climbing his minaret
To rub salt in it.

As if the sky were a wall
To listen against for voices
On the other side, arguing
About us,

Our plans for the future.
As if the piano keys were Scrabble,
And the points were chalk
On a face that turns away
So what we see

Is wood. It takes work to visualize
The canals on Mars. You have to stretch

Your imagination like a muscle
Until it hurts, and ignore
The urgent telegrams

Of *cease and desist*, bending
Your voice, like a muezzin's, to "cry
Of its occasion." It takes practice
To summon up the ghost

Of a smirk on the face
Of Princess Tatiana, doubled up in a pit
With her yellow hat and her dog,
Even if you hold hands and dance
In a circle, in the courtyard,

And the scent is of lemon trees.
As if the earth would wear us
Like a chemise, patterned
With camellias.

As if we could collect the debris
And broken glass, recycle it
Into piano scales, or a mosaic
In which a courtesan

Brandishes a tambourine against
What contains her, as if to say
Don't forget.

Quintet

Because it is pure white, you can't see
What stalks the letters. It is moving. Time
To put on the rubber suit, cock the harpoon
And fire. "A life

Of earnest contemplation," to find oneself
Impaled on a spike — as one's feet, wet
From ritual, come into contact with wire.
Jimmy claims it was a Vatican plot.

Agua hermetica was in the ink they used
To illuminate the manuscripts: prolonged exposure
Leads to watery eyes, dissolution of fingertips.
A burning in the throat, followed by choking. *God*

I miss you, and the electrodes
Attached to my gonads, to jumpstart the body
Into self-flagellatory ecstasy. For what
Would we not endure that our sky might be

A rod or a cone in the divine cathode?
And that we practice on each other in your absence,
And the fatted calf abandoned, bleeding, and Polynices
Tonguing the dust where he fell, his brother's wound

Festering in him, so that you might take offense
And visit us in the form of weather, wind
That is more than wind…

———

"A life of earnest contemplation," scanning
The wind for possible syllables, telegraphy
Out of the white noise like wave spray.
Or staring at the page in hope

The beast will stare back
From behind the cage and emit
Frightening yowl, proof of the need for poetry.

My life, like an onion, is clarified by what burns
On the other side. Time to put on the rubber suit
And dive into the funnel, for here is a whirlpool
At the very heart of contemplation, to find

Proof of the need for poetry. Can you not feel, man?
The teeth, I mean, the invisible teeth, and dissolution
Of fingertips. But they are still here, I can see them.
Yes, but are numb. Pressing the keypad,

But transmitting no syllables. More than anything
I want to attain that state of grace the instant
Before skin, wet and conducive, touches.
Moreover, the ink I use

To illuminate these letters, i.e., to heighten
So that they burn greenly in the mind, is toxic
In a subtle way, so prolonged exposure chokes.
I keep wanting to finish, it is stupid

To want to finish, for I am *a man of no fortune*
And with a name to come. Destiny is to fall
Drunkenly from the rafters into the threshing machine.
There will be no eulogy, no bronzed trophy,

But a burning in the throat, followed by choking.
Better, I think, to act out dismemberment on the page
As a stay against the frightening yowl of that beast. The cage

———————

Is all that's between us. We have been chasing each other
Around for hours now — who has enough decency
To surrender? For time, it hath a cruel harpoon,
It maketh no clean wound, but festers in the blood,

Turning thoughts crimson, like sick counsel
Of some Rasputin, staring palely at the queen in hope
Of access. Meanwhile, snap of bones

On flagstones. We have bunions to remind us
Of history. We have the potted plant
On the sill to remind us of pastoral poetry,
For which there is a proven need

No longer. Jimmy claims it was a Vatican plot,
But what does Jimmy know, festering in the tower
In which we are all imprisoned, implicated
In the conspiracy

To anoint Polynices with *agua hermetica* and jumpstart
His gonads into ecstatic spasms, beckoning forth thousands
Of flagellatory selves to penetrate the rubber suit
And gas mask of the future,

For what would we not endure that we might be
A rod or a cone in its eye?
We practice on each other in its absence.

———

A man of no fortune, and with a name to come.
Call me Ishmael — here is my cruel harpoon,
At your feet, milady. Call me Rasputin.
Here is my long nose and blistering stare,

Cataracts. Because they are pure white,
I cannot see what stalks the empire, though it is
Moving. In the privy chamber, a fatted calf
Tonguing our bunioned feet, we sit and dream up

Proof of a need for God, so we might hold
The frayed cord to his skin. When it toucheth,
Shall be frightening yowl,
Shall be poetry.

Siesta

1.

All afternoon the doves work,
little sisters of the heroines,
Cassandras too shy to speak up,
polishing their glass vowel.

2.

The sun gears up
for another world record,
once again it triumphs
infinity to nil, kicks
the streets while they're
already down, speaks
solemnly of the need
for better educational
methods, neuters
the stray cats, tells
a joke about rubber
breasts, heats the walls
until they begin
to glow from within.

3.

We found this city
of perfectly preserved
inhabitants,
plus tables of uncleared
lunches, half-drunk
Cypriot wine,
sinews of bread,
abandoned in haste
at the hour of two p.m.

4.

The month named for an emperor,
the street for a general.
Triumph of light —
one century after another has blinked in it,
gone back inside,

found a cool place to sleep. White stones,
white paint on the tree trunks,
a cat staggers out from under a car.
The land would burn,
if burning made any difference.

Silence

What more could I expect that day
at Delphi, where curious kings,
fresh from their rendezvous

with Pythia, once sat troubled
by her riddling words?
I waited out others,

a tour group making lunch plans
and consulting the map. Waited to be
the one person present,

for enough quiet to coax them
out of the woods, like deer —
naiads, demigods, whoever
might be biding their time

ever since time turned
against them, driving racers and horses
off the ellipse. I half-believed
such things as Ouija,

a plumber surprised by Caesar's
cavalry, or a place's memory
of being sacred,

long after the religion died.
Where else but here
could such things happen?

I waited. Stirring,
settling, the breeze was a vehicle
for piney scents. The hewn limestone
at ease in its decay. Nothing spoke.

www.ingramcontent.com/pod-product-compliance
Lightning Source LLC
Chambersburg PA
CBHW032132090426
42743CB00007B/577